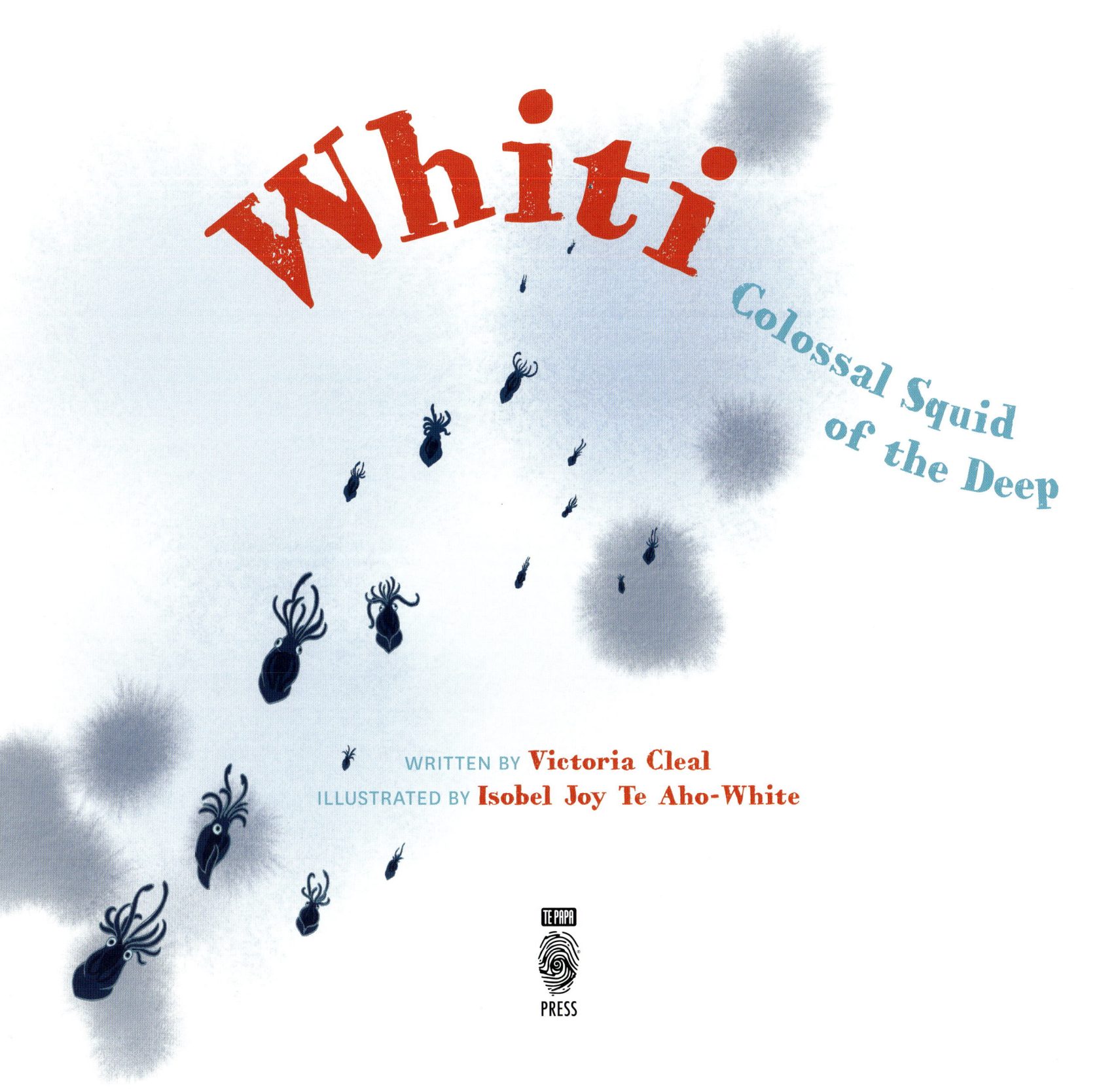

Whiti
Colossal Squid of the Deep

WRITTEN BY **Victoria Cleal**
ILLUSTRATED BY **Isobel Joy Te Aho-White**

TE PAPA PRESS

Antarctica – brrr!
Looking for a colossal squid? You've come to the right place — Antarctica.

You've travelled a long way south from Aotearoa New Zealand to here, the Ross Sea. It's about six hours in a plane across the stormy Southern Ocean.

Are you wearing lots of warm layers? Antarctica's the coldest, windiest continent on the planet. It's summer now, but it's just minus 2 degrees Celsius – colder than your fridge. In winter the temperature plummets to minus 40 degrees Celsius. That's about twice as cold as your freezer.

Almost everywhere you look, there's ice. Thin ice covers some of the Ross Sea, too. Only a small part of the land is bare of ice, and that's where Adelie penguins make their nests.

Few animals can survive in this harsh world, and those that do are built tough. As well as penguins, there are seals and seabirds, and even bugs like little springtails. Some plants live here, too – mosses, lichens and tiny algae.

CRAAACK! Now the sun's heat is breaking up the sea ice. It's time to explore underwater. Will it be as bare as above the ice? Will we spot a colossal squid?

Adelie penguins keep snug with tightly packed feathers. They stay dry by spreading waterproof oil over their feathers. On land, they waddle or sledge on their bellies over the ice.

South polar skuas are on the lookout to grab a penguin egg or chick. These incredible travellers fly to the moana (ocean) between Russia and Alaska, then back again – a journey of 34,000 kilometres every year.

Weddell seals live here all year. This mum and her pup are sunbathing by a breathing hole. Seals dive for kai (food), but they need to come up for air. Dad guards the hole. Other males don't dare to poke their snouts up here!

Snow petrels are pure white. This camouflages them against the ice, making it easier for them to hunt for ika (fish), ngū (squid) and krill. They nest further south than any bird on Earth.

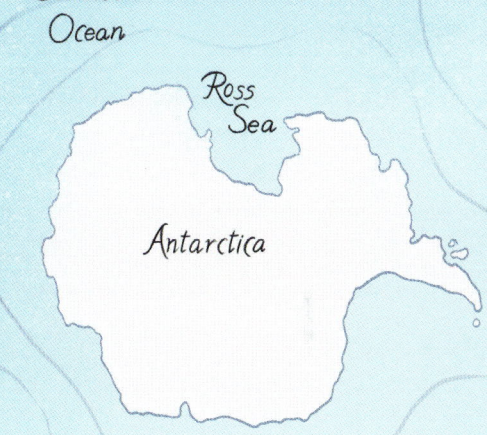

Antarctica and Aotearoa — good neighbours

The chilly waters of the Southern Ocean flow to other moana, too. They carry oxygen and nutrients that ika and other animals need to thrive. The seafood we enjoy in Aotearoa New Zealand depends on these waters – thanks, Antarctica!

Storms from the Southern Ocean reach us, too, keeping Papatūānuku, the Earth Mother, moist and cool.

Giant sea spiders aren't really spiders, but the ones in the Ross Sea do have eight legs. They can grow as big as a dinner plate, but their bodies are tiny. They have straw-like mouths to suck up the soft bits of animals.

Ready, steady, grow

The Ross Sea is fizzing with life, but summer is short. Animals here have to eat lots and grow quickly — winter will soon be back.

See how the ice is a greenish colour underneath? It's covered in tiny plants called algae – they're the start of this explosion of life. Algae need light to grow, and right now they're getting it 24 hours a day. In summer, the sun doesn't set in Antarctica.

Millions of shrimp-like krill gobble up the algae. Ika, penguins and many other animals gorge on the krill. Then those animals become kai for seals.

The mauri (life force) is strong here in the sunlight zone (0 to 200 metres deep). The temperature of the wai (water) is minus 1.8 degrees Celsius all year, and only its saltiness stops it from freezing. But these animals can cope with cold.

Plankton (tiny plants and animals) float in the moana. Sometimes, blooms of plant plankton grow so huge that they can be seen from space.

There are even tiny colossal squid here – can you spot them?

Watch out, babies

Newborn colossal squid are a tasty meal for many animals. Being see-through helps them hide — but only a lucky few will survive.

These bulgy-eyed babies hatched from ant-sized eggs. Cute! Now they're as big as your thumb. Their fins are too tiny for swimming, so they pump wai out their tube-like funnels to push themselves along. They poo out of the funnels, too.

These little invertebrates gobble whatever they can grab, like animal plankton. And *they* get gobbled, too! Penguins, ika and lots of other animals love to eat tender baby ngū.

It's hard to hide from hunters in the moana, but baby colossal squid have a few neat tricks. They probably squirt ink out their funnels to confuse predators, and they're hard to spot. They're a type of glass squid, and are almost totally see-through.

Not everyone's fooled though. Uh-oh! A young toothfish just nabbed some babies.

This Antarctic minke whale's chasing krill – but it might scoop up tiny ngū, too. Swim, babies!

One ngū called Whiti escapes. Phew, that was close.

Who needs a backbone?

The sea floor under the ice swarms with colourful invertebrates – animals that don't have backbones. Can you feel your backbone? You're a vertebrate, like fish and birds.

Antarctic silverfish

Brittle stars look like sea stars, but they're skinnier. Their wriggly arms allow them to move fast.

This *Antarctic minke whale* gulps in wai, then pushes it out between bristly plates called baleen. The bristles strain out the wai and trap little animals like krill.

baleen

Ika that thrive in ice

Most ika would freeze solid into a fishblock if they touched ice, and that's everywhere here. Some ika in the Antarctic have a secret weapon – chemicals in their blood stop ice growing in their bodies.

Icefish have gone even further. They're the only ika in the world with no red blood cells (which make blood thicker). Without red blood cells, the icefish's blood flows more easily in the chilly wai.

icefish

Glowing in the dark

Whiti's grown big — soon she'll start moving into the deep. It's dark there, but Whiti's eyes are like headlights!

She travels down through the twilight zone (200 to 1,000 metres deep). Only a tiny bit of light reaches this far.

Deeper … deeper … Now she's in the midnight zone (1,000 to 4,000 metres deep). This is where Whiti will live from now on – in darkness.

Imagine swimming around down here. All you'd see of Whiti would be lights beaming from around her karu (eyes). This is bioluminescence – light made by living things. The light may help her spot prey and figure out how far away it is.

Whiti sees better than any animal in the deep. Her karu are the biggest in the world, the size of soccer balls! The pupils of these enormous karu are as large as apples. They let in 144 times more light than your pupils. Daylight would now be agony for Whiti.

But down here, those sharp karu see all prey. And she's about to attack …

lanternfish

Lights of the deep

Most animals in the deep make light, to look for one another or for dinner.

Lanternfish flash patterns of light from their bellies. That's how they find their own species among all the other lanternfish. Millions of lanternfish swim up nearer the moana surface every night to feed. It's like a galaxy of moving stars.

Hooked!

Whiti's now a top hunter. There's no way to escape her huge, swivelling hooks.

She spends most of her time watching for kai. She doesn't chase ika and smaller ngū, but waits for them to come to her.

She spots lanternfish – they're tasty. Whiti gets ready to attack …

Wait. A toothfish glides up. That's one huge meal! But a feisty toothfish can take a serious chunk out of a colossal squid. Is it worth the fight?

Whiti lifts her arms to see it better. It's big, but not too big.

She tenses, then lunges and fires out her tentacles. Gotcha!

The tentacles' hooks snag the toothfish. Whiti grabs it with her eight arms and hauls it in. The toothfish thrashes, but it's totally wrapped in her strong arms.

Whiti gobbles the toothfish the way you'd eat a corn cob.

Colossal squid have eight arms, each with two rows of suckers and sharp hooks in the middle. Most suckers have sharp, pointy 'teeth' to grip victims. A few suckers have spikes instead of teeth – another way to snag prey.

As well as eight arms, colossal squid have two tentacles. These grow up to 2 metres long in adults – longer than the height of most human adults. The clubs at the end have big hooks that are the size of a $2 coin. These hooks can twist right round. The colossal squid is the only known ngū with swivelling hooks.

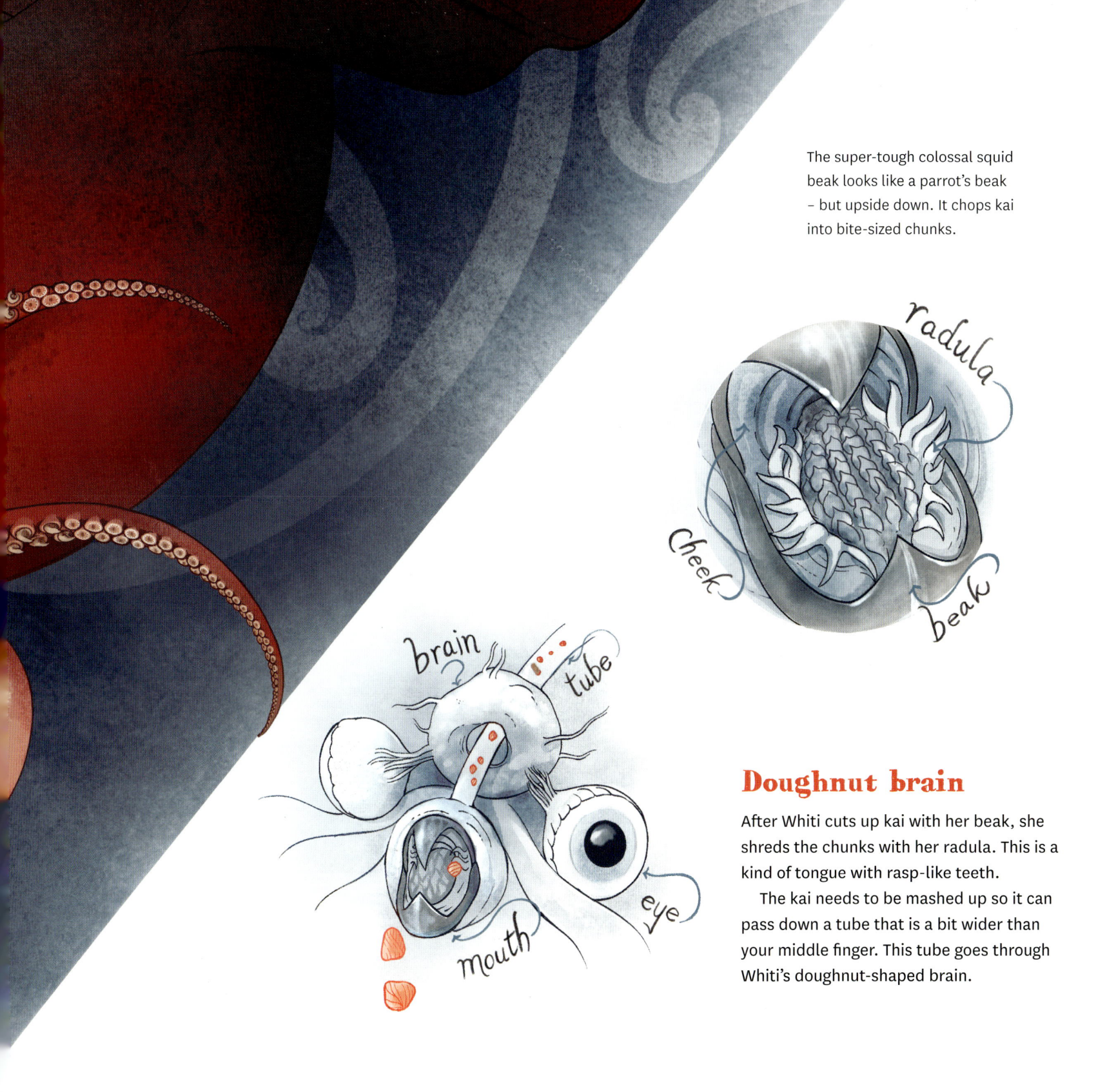

The super-tough colossal squid beak looks like a parrot's beak – but upside down. It chops kai into bite-sized chunks.

Doughnut brain

After Whiti cuts up kai with her beak, she shreds the chunks with her radula. This is a kind of tongue with rasp-like teeth.

The kai needs to be mashed up so it can pass down a tube that is a bit wider than your middle finger. This tube goes through Whiti's doughnut-shaped brain.

What a whopper

Whiti's fully grown, and enormous — a world record holder!

Remember the invertebrates you saw under the ice on the sea floor, like sea stars? Whiti is now the most massive invertebrate in the world. Her mantle is the length of a cow – 2.5 metres. With her tentacles stretched out, she's the length of a car – 4.5 metres. She weighs 500 kilograms, as much as six human adults. You wouldn't want to mess with this hefty ngū.

Why does a colossal squid become, well, colossal? We don't know. One thing's for sure – when you're as big as a colossal squid, there aren't many other animals big enough to eat you. You're at the top of the food chain.

Even though she is huge, Whiti is graceful. Look at her cruising along. To see better, she bunches her arms up in a 'cockatoo' pose – like a cockatoo's head feathers sticking up. She ripples her fins to move, steers with her funnel, and mostly goes backwards!

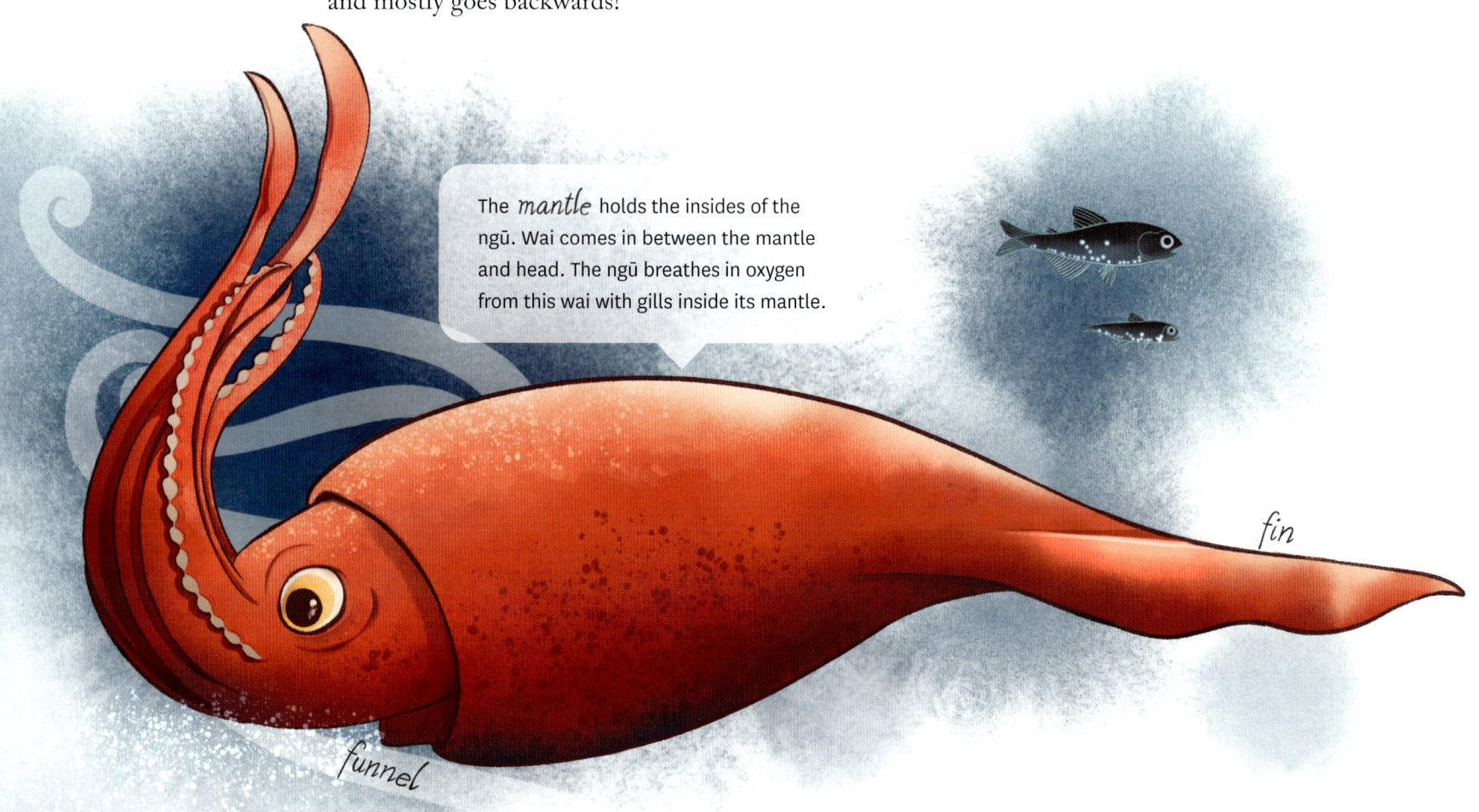

The *mantle* holds the insides of the ngū. Wai comes in between the mantle and head. The ngū breathes in oxygen from this wai with gills inside its mantle.

giant jelly

Under pressure

The deeper you go in the moana, the greater the pressure, or force, of wai pressing down on you. How does the colossal squid survive the tremendous pressures at depths of 1,000 to 2,000 metres?

Pressure is mainly a problem for animals with air spaces in their bodies, especially when they move up and down quickly in the wai. If you were diving down to Whiti's world, the pressure would shrink the air in your body. Your lungs would cave in – like a balloon with the air sucked out of it.

But a colossal squid doesn't have air spaces, and doesn't move up and down quickly. Whiti can handle the pressure!

Hiding with red

Colossal squid become red as they get older. Whiti can change from pink to dark red. In the deep, it's the perfect colour for hiding from predators or prey.

Red stands out in our light-filled world – think of pōhutukawa flowers. But red light can't reach far down in wai. Red animals in the deep just look black, like the wai around them. They're pretty much invisible.

Lots of deep-sea creatures are red, like this giant jelly. Most jellies have stinging tentacles to protect themselves from predators, but this one doesn't bother. Instead, its red colour keeps it hidden – even though it's twice as long as the colossal squid!

Treat or trap?

A juicy toothfish hangs in the moana, ready to be gobbled up — is this too good to be true?

Ice covered the whole of the Ross Sea in winter. Now it is spring again, and the ice will soon break up. Down in Whiti's dark world, though, it's hard to tell the seasons apart. The temperature stays the same all year. But spring brings a surprise …

Whiti discovers the biggest toothfish she's ever seen. It has become caught on something and died. This victim won't struggle – perfect!

She grabs the ika and starts munching. Mmm, it's still fresh.

The toothfish is hooked on a longline, reeled down 1,500 metres from a fishing boat. For a few months each year, fishers from Aotearoa and other countries come here. They catch toothfish only in the northern Ross Sea, and they're not allowed to take too many.

The line's moving up. The boat's hauling the toothfish in. Should Whiti keep feasting or let go?

Long before she was born, another colossal squid didn't let go of a hooked toothfish. That one became world famous …

Toothfish — in no rush

For toothfish, slow's the way to go. They're not fast movers, and their hearts beat just six times a minute. (Your heart beats about ninety times a minute.) They grow slowly, too, and can live for nearly fifty years. Some toothfish are longer than you are tall!

The Ross Sea's special killer whales

Kākahi (killer whales) are actually dolphins. Most kākahi in Antarctica eat whales, seals and penguins.

Some kākahi in the Ross Sea are different – they mainly eat toothfish and other ika. These super-smart predators hunt together for ika under the pack ice.

This type of kākahi connects Antarctica to Aotearoa. They can swim all the way to Northland, a trip that takes about three weeks.

kākahi killer whales

Squid celebrity

Humans were astonished by the biggest colossal squid ever found. Now she's a star at Te Papa.

Way back in 2007, the New Zealand fishing boat *San Aspiring* hauled up a colossal squid in the Ross Sea. She was dying, and couldn't be saved.

The crew knew this was an amazing find – an almost fully grown colossal squid in good shape. Earlier, people had found beaks and other body parts in whale and ika stomachs. But a whole colossal squid was incredibly rare.

What would you do with a dead colossal squid? The crew froze this ngū into a cube like an iceblock, and sent her to Te Papa in Wellington.

Scientists at the national museum and around the world were excited about this *Mesonychoteuthis hamiltoni* (the colossal squid's scientific name). But how could they safely defrost a 'squidblock' weighing 495 kilograms?

The experts filled a tank with saltwater, added some saltwater ice and defrosted the ngū at 10 degrees Celsius. Success! Then, they carefully cut her open to study her body parts. Next, they put her in a bath of chemicals to stop her from rotting. Finally, they built a special tank with a glass lid and lowered her in. Now she was ready to be put on display.

This is the only whole colossal squid on display in the world! Millions of people have visited her.

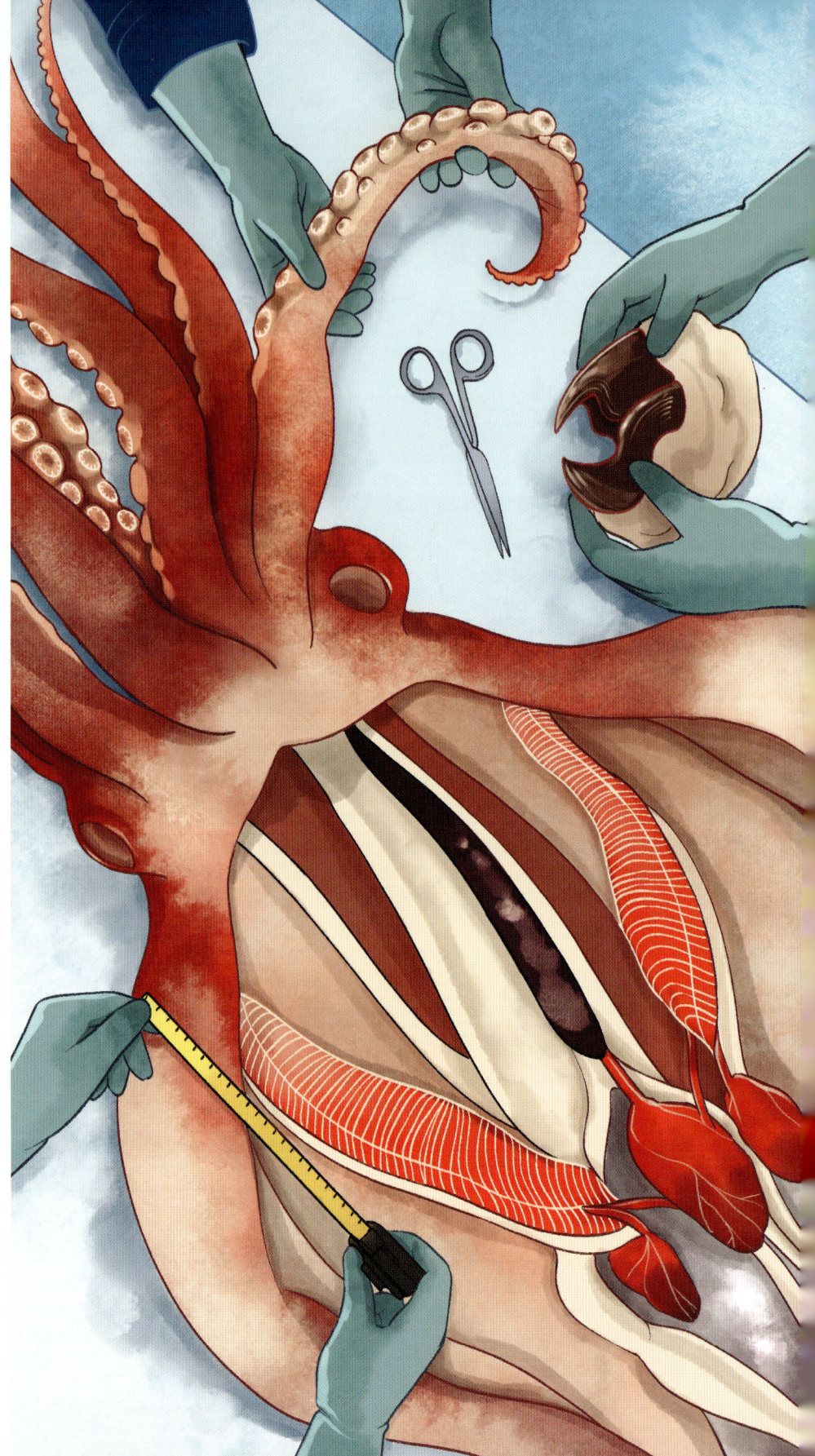

Oops – we left our ngū hanging on that longline. Whiti's getting hauled into the twilight zone. There's too much light for her huge karu. She lets go of the toothfish and sinks back into the deep.

Te Papa's squid stash

Te Papa actually has four colossal squid, but the other three aren't in such good shape. The museum also has six giant squid, and thousands of other ngū and their relatives – some are whole, while others are just bits.

They can't all be displayed – that would take up loads of room. Instead, they're stored in another building. The colossal and giant squids are in steel tanks the size of ten bathtubs. Smaller species are in jars or plastic buckets. All are kept in special preserving liquids.

Scientists study the ngū to understand more about these animals and their world.

A whale on the trail

Summer brings male parāoa (sperm whales) to Antarctica. They can dive 2,000 metres for their favourite kai — colossal squid.

Whiti is now ruler of her deep world. Only one Antarctic animal can take on a healthy colossal squid. That's the southern sleeper shark, and Whiti hasn't come across one. Life's sweet for our ngū, right?

Not quite. Far above her, a visitor arrives … a parāoa bigger than a bus.

This parāoa is a mammal, like us humans, and needs to breathe air. At the surface, he takes a deep breath – enough air to last two hours. He closes his blowhole, tilts up his tail and dives.

The pressure builds. The air in the parāoa's lungs shrinks, but his ribcage sinks in to help him cope. His heart slows. He swims deeper. He can't see in the dark. How will he find prey?

He sends out clicks as sound waves. Tik … tik … tik … The sound waves bounce off Whiti and back to the parāoa. He can tell there's a big meal below.

Tik, tik, tik … He's getting close. His clicks speed up. Tik-tik-tik-tik-tik-tik-tik-tik … He ploughs through bioluminescent animals towards the colossal squid.

Whiti sees the animals scatter. She knows something huge is coming. Move, Whiti, move!

TIKTIKTIKTIKTIKTIKTIKTIKTIKTIKTIK

The parāoa opens his jaws. Whiti lunges sideways. The parāoa sucks in – and grabs a smaller squid in his teeth instead. He swallows it whole. There's no time left to chase Whiti. He needs to go up for air.

Whiti is one lucky ngū.

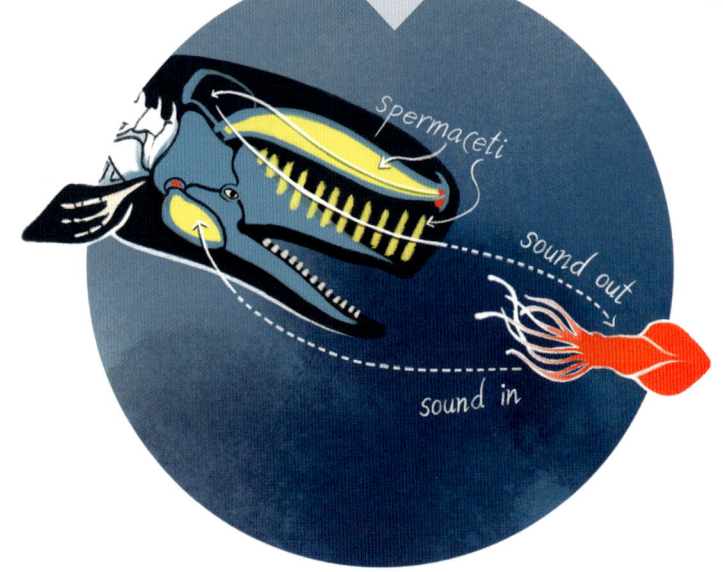

The chunky *head* of a parāoa (sperm whale) is filled with an oily liquid called spermaceti. The spermaceti focuses the parāoa's clicks into a beam of sound waves. The beam bounces off objects and comes back to him. This is echolocation – it's like seeing with sound.

Precious parāoa

Māori and other Pacific peoples are closely connected to whales and see them as tuākana (elders) of the moana. Many iwi (tribes) tell stories about whales that guided waka (canoes) to Aotearoa from Hawaiki, homeland of the ancestors. Some brave ancestors even rode whales!

For hundreds of years, Māori have watched parāoa journey past Aotearoa to Antarctica. Sometimes, parāoa beach themselves by accident and die.

For Māori, these stranded parāoa are a gift from Tangaroa, god of the moana. Their meat was once important kai for protein. Today, their bones and teeth are still carved to make treasures like musical instruments and neck pendants. This modern nguru (nose flute) even looks like a parāoa with a spiral-shaped head.

Secret date

Whiti is looking for a mate. How she gets one is a mystery.

Whiti's now old enough to have babies, but first she needs a male.

How does a colossal squid find another colossal squid in the dark? We don't know the answer to this.

Do groups of them hang out together sometimes? Or do they just bump into each other now and then? We don't know that either.

We don't even know what a male colossal squid looks like! Nobody's ever found a fully grown one. What do you think he'd look like?

There's still so much to find out about life deep in the Ross Sea. Humans have been to the Moon, but nobody has ever been down to Whiti's world. Many other strange animals that have never been seen before might live down there.

Only a tiny part of the world's moana has been thoroughly explored.

Amazing discoveries

It's only since 2004 that we've started to learn about life deep in the Ross Sea. New Zealand scientists have lowered video cameras from moving boats to film down there. They've put nets into the moana and onto the sea floor, and scooped up animals to study. Some exciting creatures have been hauled up!

The *snailfish* has bendy bones and a jelly-like body to cope with deep-sea pressure. Some species of snailfish live deeper than any other ika. This species can be found nearly 2,000 metres below the surface of the Ross Sea.

This *wheke octopus* is called the dumbo octopus. It is named after the make-believe big-eared elephant called Dumbo. Those bumps on its head aren't ears though, but little fins for swimming and steering. It's sometimes called the umbrella octopus. Can you see why? This species was found 3,000 metres deep – even deeper than colossal squid live.

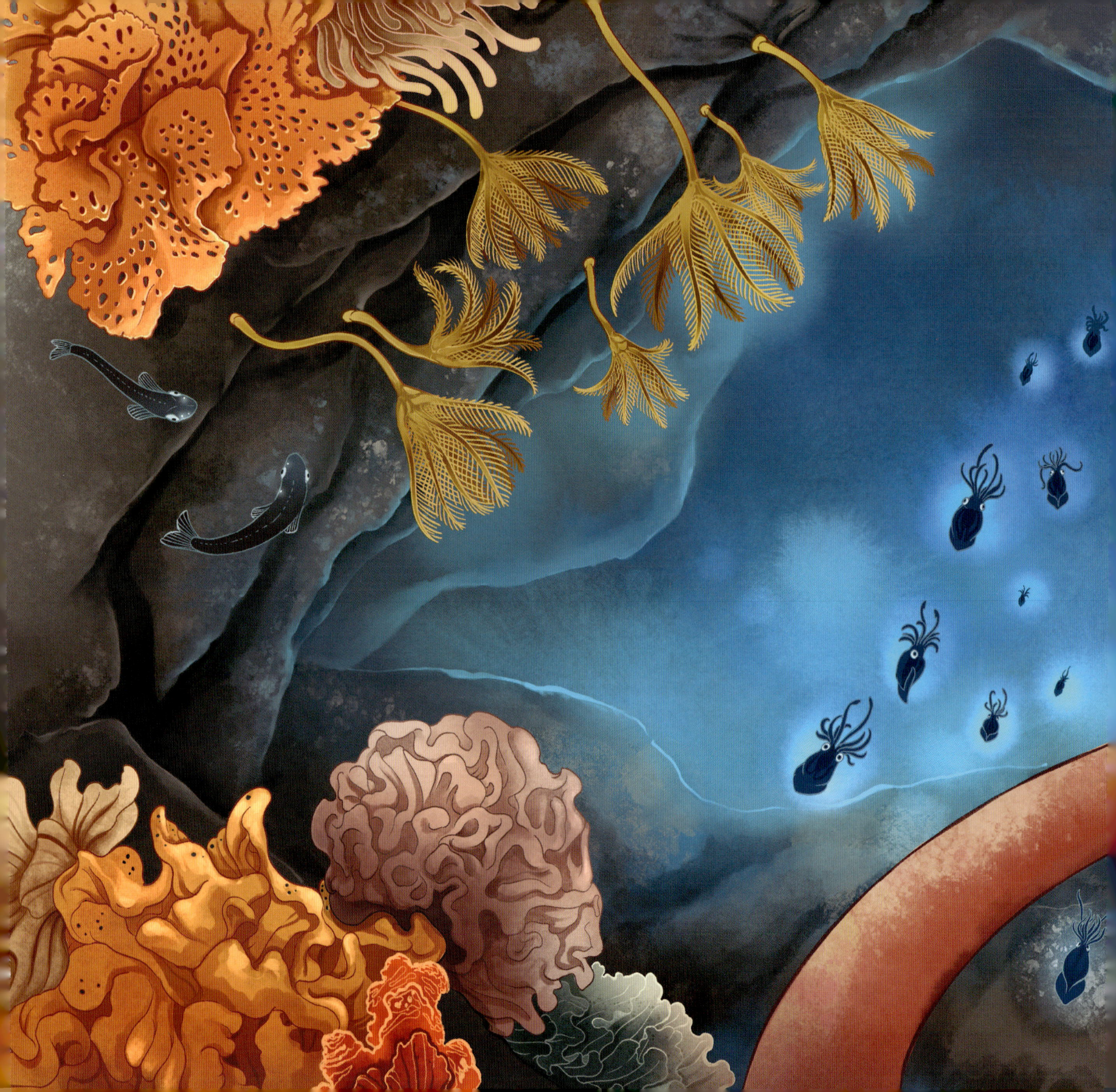

Goodbye, Whiti

Our ngū has found a mate and laid thousands of eggs. Now she will die — but the cycle of life goes on.

Like all female ngū, Whiti stopped eating after she laid her eggs. She won't live much longer.

We don't know how old she is. Other ngū live less than two years, but a colossal squid might live longer.

Haere rā, e Whiti – goodbye!

A colossal squid's body is a great gift for Ross Sea animals. The body floats to the surface, to the light. It is kai for penguins, toothfish, whales, seals, albatrosses and other seabirds. Some pieces sink down again and feed animals that live on the sea floor, like the invertebrates here.

The Ross Sea might seem like a tough world, but all living things here are in balance. Its mauri is healthy.

And already, a bunch of Whiti's babies are about to start their own adventures. Good luck!

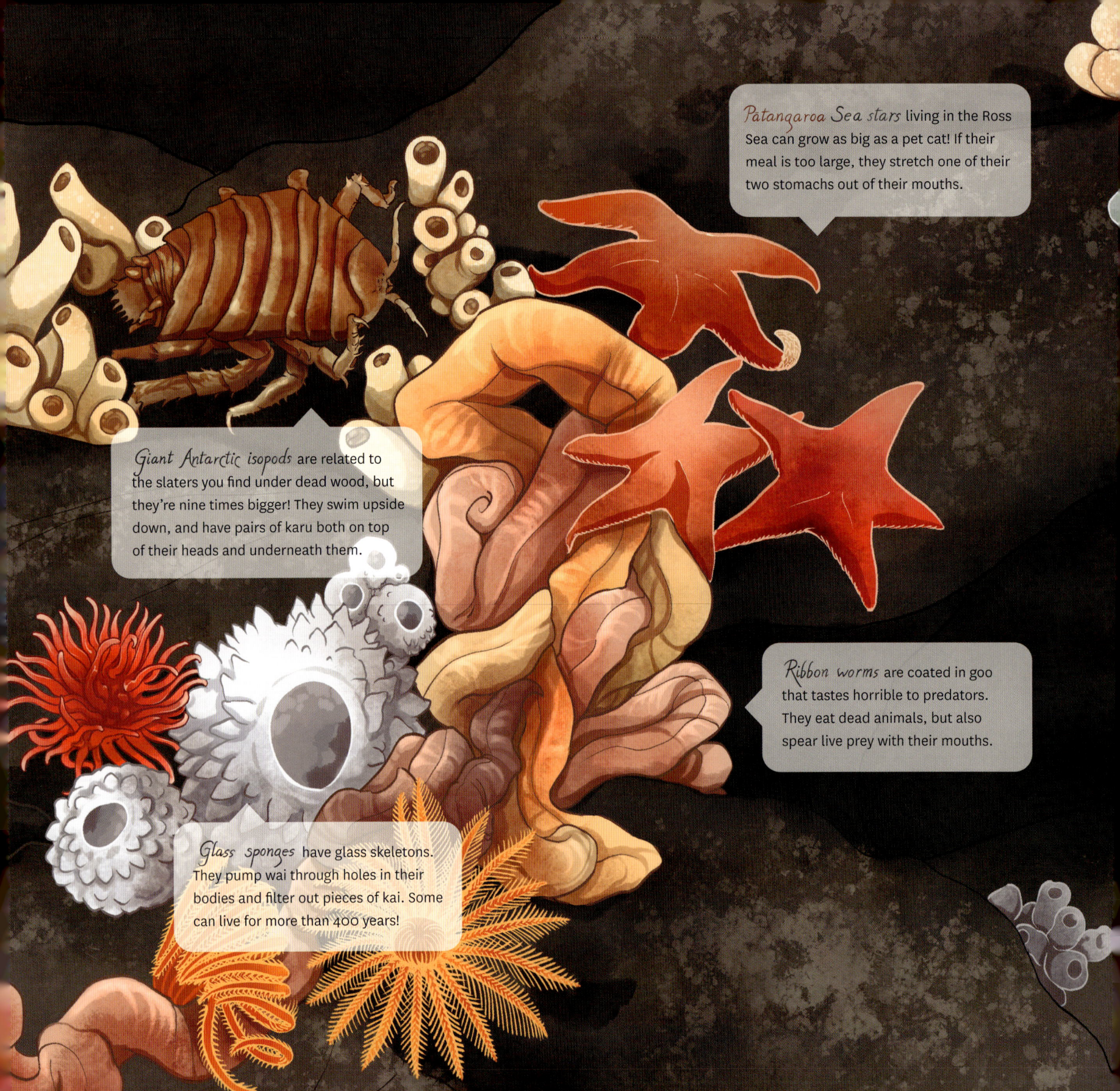

Poo for dinner — yum!

Some animals on the sea floor gather kai from the wai. A lot of this is 'marine snow' that drifts down from above. Marine snow looks like real snow, but it's actually tiny bits of dead creatures and plants, and animal poo.

Some of these bits land on the sea floor and turn into mud. Animals like sea cucumbers guzzle this mud – they're the vacuum cleaners of the moana.

Every scrap of kai here is precious – nothing's wasted.

Sea pigs look like water balloons on legs, but they're a type of sea cucumber. Like real pigs, they love wallowing in mud. They feed by picking up the mud with tentacles round their mouths.

The legs of *king crabs* can be as long as your legs. King crabs grab pieces of kai with their claws and pass them into their mouths.

Antarctica's guardians

This icy continent is so special that countries all around the world care for it — and learn from it.

Aotearoa New Zealand and many other countries have agreed to be the kaitiaki (guardians) of Antarctica and keep its mauri strong. New Zealand helped make a big part of the Ross Sea a marine protected area. It's now a safe place in the moana for plants and animals. That's good news for colossal squid!

Different countries have about forty bases dotted around Antarctica. New Zealand's is Scott Base, on Ross Island. It has a gym, a library and even a shop. All rubbish and recycling is shipped out — that's part of being good kaitiaki.

In summer, scientists arrive at Scott Base. People who support them come, too, like chefs, drivers and pilots. The scientists want to understand how Antarctica and the rest of the world affect each other. They study Antarctica's ice, weather, moana, plants and animals.

Humans are changing the world's climate. We're creating too much carbon dioxide and other greenhouse gases. Scientists want to know if that will make Antarctica's moana warmer. Could it melt the massive ice sheets, too? That would raise sea levels everywhere.

The things these scientists learn in Antarctica can teach us about the effects climate change might have around the world.

Science under the ice

Imagine working in wai that's minus 1.8 degrees Celsius! First, you put on a suit that is like a sleeping bag, then a waterproof drysuit on top. You attach weights so you won't bob to the surface. Finally, you slip on scuba gear.

You slide through a hole in the ice. Don't worry, you won't get lost – you're tied to this hole. Your drysuit will keep your body warm, but your lips and hands will soon go numb.

Sound fun? Scientists who dive under the ice think they're lucky. Not many people get to see this wonderful world.

See the scallops this scientist is collecting? She'll test them to see if changes in the moana could harm their shells.

Scallops need calcium to grow their shells. Many other animals need calcium, too, like sea stars, kina and some corals.

But climate change means that the moana is absorbing more carbon dioxide. This chemical change makes it harder for animals to get calcium from the wai.

Squid

Giant squid

Colossal

Meet the colossal squid's family
Ngū are related to wheke (octopuses), cuttlefish and nautiluses — spot the differences!

They're all cephalopods, a word that means their arms come out of their heads.

They're weirdly built in other ways, too. All cephalopods apart from the nautilus have three hearts, and their blood is blue. By growing and shrinking dots of colour on their bodies, they can change their appearance to lure mates and scare away predators.

All cephalopods have a mantle, a funnel, gills, a beak and a tongue-like radula. Most squirt ink, have amazing eyesight, and can feel and taste with their suckers. They're the brainiest invertebrates, too – although you're still way smarter than they are!

Cephalopods are a type of mollusc – like the snails in your garden. Shellfish like pāua and mussels are molluscs, too. They all have soft bodies, and many have shells. Even the colossal squid has a small shell hidden inside – it's long and thin like a leaf.

Nautiluses have no arms, but they have about ninety tentacles. They cruise around in a big shell. Gas in the shell helps the nautilus float.

Cuttlefish have eight arms and two tentacles like ngū, but their bodies are flatter and chunkier. The pupils of their karu are shaped like the letter W.

Wheke Octopuses have eight arms and no tentacles. Most of the time they crawl around, feeling and gripping with their suckers. They can change colour to blend in with the sea floor – handy for hiding from predators. Some can even make their skin bumpy like rock!

This is a fossil of an **ammonite**, an ancient cephalopod. This ammonite species lived around Aotearoa about 140 million years ago. The fossil weighs a tonne, and it had to be blown out of rock with explosives! It's now at Te Papa.

Ngū Squid have eight arms and two tentacles with suckers, hooks or both. Some adults are the size of your little finger! Humboldt squid like this one live in groups that can number 1,200 or more. They send each other messages with 'flashes' – changing colour from red to white super fast.

Colossal vs giant squid

Long before people knew about the colossal squid, they were terrified of the giant squid. It's probably the animal that European sailors called the Kraken. They told wild stories about it attacking whole ships.

Which is the biggest?

Colossal squid

Longest
4.2 metres

Heaviest
495 kilograms – winner!

Biggest karu
30 centimetres – it's a tie! –

Giant squid

Longest
13 metres – winner!

Heaviest
275 kilograms

Biggest karu
30 centimetres

They're both champions!

The measurements above are for the biggest colossal squid and giant squid ever found. But even larger ones could lurk in the moana!

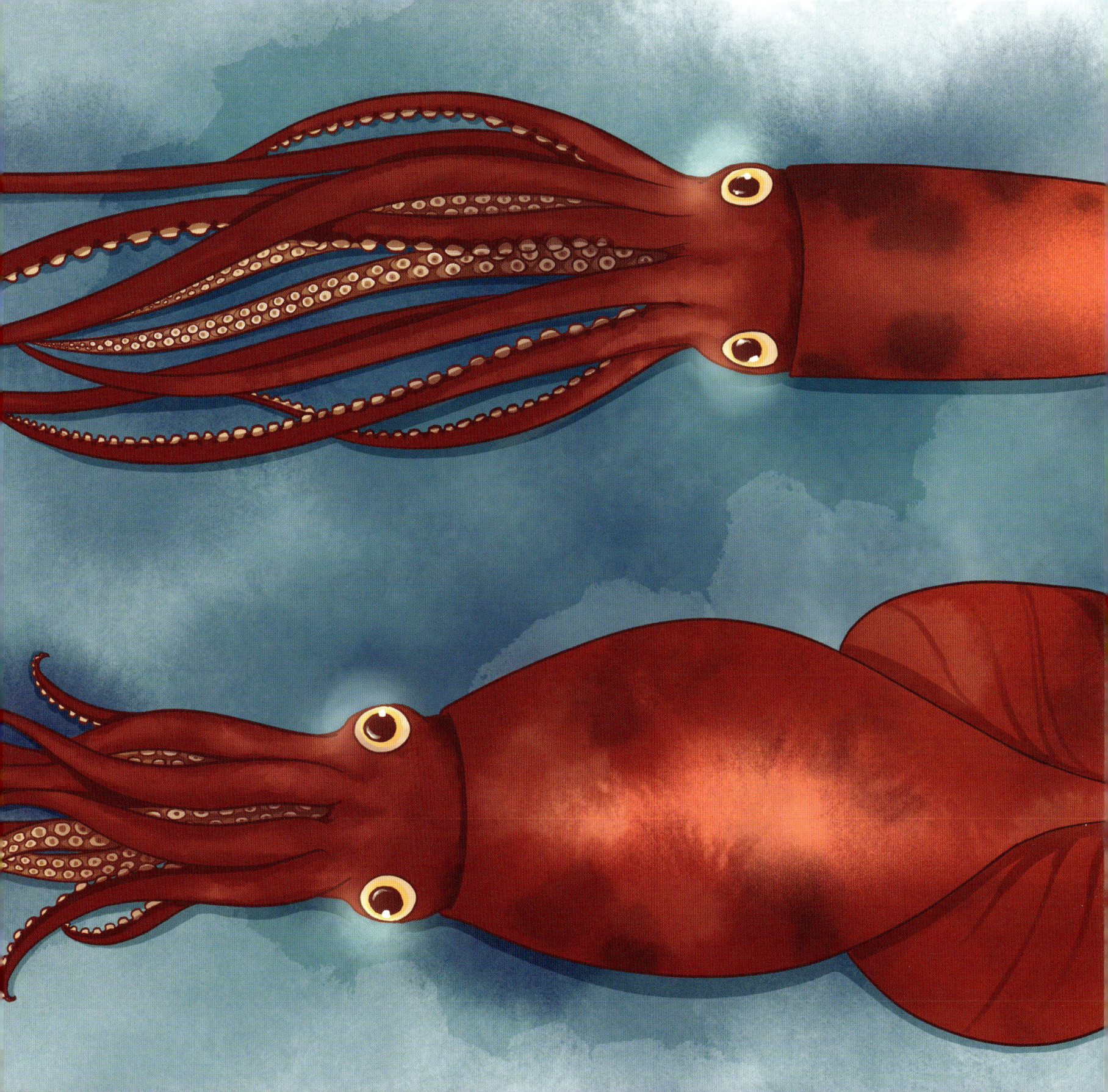

Ngū and wheke near you

They're all around Aotearoa. If you're lucky, you might see a live one.

We have more than ninety species of ngū but most live far out in the moana. Aotearoa is home to about forty-two species of wheke, too. Cuttlefish and nautiluses don't live near New Zealand.

If you snorkel, you may see a live ngū, although you're more likely to see just a puff of ink as it scoots away! Check kelp for 'egg mops' – these are clusters of broad-squid eggs.

Have a search in rock pools for young wheke. They're good at blending in, so look closely for their karu.

Do you live near a west coast beach? Look for the spiral shells of the ram's horn squid. This shell is inside its body and helps the animal float.

Giant squid wash up on our coasts, too. They live in the deep all around the world.

Next time you're on a coast, look across the moana of Tangaroa. Wai from Antarctica that colossal squid once swam in is mixed into that moana. We're not so far from Antarctica after all.

The members of this whānau (family) are *kaitiaki* of the moana. They're picking up plastic rubbish so it doesn't end up in the wai. Sea animals can eat plastic and become sick or die. You and your whānau can help keep beaches and rivers clean, too.

Kupe and Wheke

It's said that Kupe was a fisher in Hawaiki, surrounded by the warm Pacific Ocean. A massive wheke, Te Wheke a Muturangi, kept stealing the bait from his fishing lines. Kupe was pretty fed up. 'I'm going to catch Wheke!' he exclaimed. He got two waka ready, and set out in chase with his whānau and friends.

For weeks, Wheke led them across the moana, to a strange, cloudy land – Aotearoa. Kupe's people were great navigators though, and they caught up with Wheke at Cook Strait.

They threw spears, but Wheke snapped the weapons like twigs. He reached his arms round the waka to pull them underwater. 'Throw the hue overboard!' Kupe yelled. The water gourds bobbed in the moana. To Wheke, they looked like heads. He lunged at them floating on the surface – and Kupe killed him with one blow.

About the author

Victoria Cleal is a writer and editor at Te Papa. That's been handy for writing this book, as there is a real colossal squid at her workplace and she gets to meet many passionate (and patient) scientists. Recently, Victoria has written digital labels for Te Papa's Te Taiao | Nature zone and stories from the book *Māui's Taonga Tales*.

About the illustrator

Isobel Joy Te Aho-White (Ngāti Kahungunu, Kāi Tahu) is a graphic artist with a Diploma in Visual Arts from the Universal College of Learning (UCOL) and a Bachelor of Design (Hons) majoring in illustration from Massey University. Izzy lives and works in Te Whanganui-a-Tara (Wellington), where she is inspired by an eclectic range of artists, old and new. She has a passion for educational and storybook illustration, and her work often incorporates themes that are important to her – te ao Māori, kaitiakitanga, environmentalism and a connection to the natural world. Izzy feels at home in the dark and has a particular soft spot for all things creepy and crawly.

Dr Kat Bolstad (left) examines a colossal squid at Te Papa, 2014.

Acknowledgements

The author and illustrator wish to thank the following people for their generous assistance.

- Museum of New Zealand Te Papa Tongarewa (Te Papa): Rodrigo Salvador, Curator Invertebrates; Andrew Stewart, Assistant Curator Vertebrates; Thomas Schultz, Kaitiaki Taonga Collection Manager; Felix Marx, Curator Vertebrates; Ranea Aperahama (Mōrehu), Kaituhi Māori
- Auckland University of Technology (AUT) Lab for Cephalopod Ecology and Systematics: Associate Professor Kathrin Bolstad; Dr Aaron Evans
- National Institute of Water and Atmospheric Research (NIWA): Kareen Schnabel, Marine Biologist; Sadie Mills, Principal Technician, Marine Biology; Di Tracey, Fisheries Scientist; Peter Marriott, Principal Technician, Marine Biology; Natalie Robinson, Marine Physicist; Darren Stevens, Fisheries Scientist; Michelle Kelly, Marine Biologist
- David Brechin-Smith
- Lauren Schaer, writer
- Francis and Hugo Coulter, and Maya Holland, amazing readers
- Bradford Haami (Ngāti Awa, Ngāti Kahungunu, Kāi Tahu, Tūwharetoa), author, lecturer, Māori historian
- Antarctica New Zealand: Georgia Nelson, Communications Advisor
- Fayne Robinson (Kāi Tahu)
- Rangi Kipa (Taranaki, Te Atiawa Nui Tonu, Ngāti Maniapoto), sculptor, carver, illustrator, tā moko artist

Kupu (Māori words)

Hue Gourd
Ika Fish
Iwi Tribe
Kai Food
Kaitiaki Guardian
Kākahi Killer whale
Karu Eye
Mauri Life force
Moana Ocean
Ngū Squid
Nguru Nose flute
Papatūānuku Earth Mother
Parāoa Sperm whale
Tangaroa Ocean god
Tuākana Elders
Wai Water
Waka Canoe
Whānau Family
Wheke Octopus

Words for colossal squid fans

Alga	Type of plant that lives in or near water	**Molluscs**	Group of animals that includes cephalopods, snails and shellfish
Baleen	Plates that filter food in a baleen whale's mouth	**Nutrient**	Chemical that a living thing needs for growth and health
Bioluminescence	Light made by living things	**Plankton**	Tiny animals and plants that drift in open water
Cephalopod	Squid, octopuses, cuttlefish, nautiluses and their relatives	**Predator**	Animal that kills and eats other animals
Echolocation	Locating things with reflected sound	**Pressure**	Force or weight that is pressing on an object
Food chain	Series of living things that eat the next in the series for food	**Prey**	Animal that is killed for food
Funnel	Tube-shaped muscle for jet swimming and squirting out ink and waste	**Radula**	Tongue-like body part in molluscs used for eating
Gill	Body part of many water animals that they use to breathe	**Spermaceti**	Oily liquid in a sperm whale's head
Greenhouse gases	Carbon dioxide and other gases that are warming the Earth's air	**Sucker**	Cup-like body part that an animal uses to feel or grip objects
Invertebrate	Animal with no backbone	**Tentacle**	Long, thin body part that an animal uses to feel or grab objects
Krill	Small shrimp-like animals	**Vertebrate**	Animal with a backbone
Mantle	The body part that covers a mollusc's insides		

First published in New Zealand in 2020 by
Te Papa Press, PO Box 467, Wellington, New Zealand
www.tepapapress.co.nz

Text © Victoria Cleal
Images © Isobel Joy Te Aho-White

This book is copyright. Apart from any fair dealing for the purpose of private study, research, criticism, or review, as permitted under the Copyright Act, no part of this book may be reproduced by any process, stored in a retrieval system, or transmitted in any form, without the prior permission of the Museum of New Zealand Te Papa Tongarewa.

TE PAPA® is the trademark of the Museum of New Zealand Te Papa Tongarewa
Te Papa Press is an imprint of the Museum of New Zealand Te Papa Tongarewa

A catalogue record is available from the National Library of New Zealand
ISBN 978-0-9951338-0-8

Design by Kate Barraclough
Printed by 1010 Printing Asia Limited, China